ALSO BY SAMUEL RAHBERG

Enduring Ministry: Toward a Lifetime of Christian Leadership (author)

The Gospels in Poem and Image (with artist Natalie Rahberg)

The Way Forward: A Collection of Benedictine Inspirations (editor)

Illuminating Ministry: A Journal, Vol. 3 (contributor)

Cover art by Natalie Rahberg | www.paintingsandmurals.com
Photo of Samuel Rahberg by John Doman
ISBN: 0-9989657-2-3
ISBN-13: 978-0-9989657-2-7

ICE BREAK

Samuel Rahberg

AETOS PUBLICATIONS
SAINT PAUL, MINNESOTA

For love,
in all its beautiful
ambiguities.

CONTENTS

Introduction   7

I   Ice Break   11

II   Anima   27

III   Holy Listening   41

IV   Yokefellows   57

V   Before God   73

VI   Woodland Love   89

About the Author   105

ACKNOWLEDGEMENTS

These poems and my life are stronger
thanks to Victor Klimoski and Kiely Todd Roska,
my companions in holy, colorful words.

INTRODUCTION

Every writer has a particular reason for setting pen to paper. Let me share mine: I want to remember moments that feel holy, moments that feel like they are changing me. Too often I am touched to the core—through beauty, persons, or discovery—only to return within minutes to my old worries and my old ways. I write to linger with precious moments long enough to carve out some memory for my future self and for others. Writing helps me leave markers of gratitude along the winding trail of blessings and growth that I can only recognize in hindsight.

When I write, sometimes it's enough for me to capture the briefest inkling as a reminder—a world made fresh with the first snow, some piece of music that stirs my soul, or a mother in poverty who admirably conveys dignity and the capacity to dream. Like smells from childhood, these poems fill my heart with stories. At other times, staying at the process of writing and refining a poem invites a moment to keep dancing with my imagination until my awareness and hope begin to brighten. Then returning to these poems, as much as writing them, honors and feeds my desire to live more deeply from the moments that have held the power to shape me.

These years have seen many moments and many poems. The sheer volume of those experiences reminds me that there is always more to learn on life's journey and that the pace of growth and change is often slow and barely noticeable.

As much as I would prefer the blaze of authenticity to ignite swiftly and burn vigorously, my experience continues to teach me a different pattern. Real and lasting change doesn't seem to come like a burst of flame as often as it comes like ice, slowly and humbly melting toward water.

Coming home to the humble and familiar way of slow change is the theme of the title poem and this collection, *Ice Break*. Like frozen top waters just beginning to crack and thaw, we depend on moments of sunshine and warmth or pressure and collision to help the process of change along. The thickest ice lasts long after temperatures rise above freezing. As lake ice melts, it does not usually go quietly. It rumbles and cracks, bit by bit, until it sinks into warmer waters or blows in sheets toward shore. Such are the realities of slow change as I know them—not smooth and comfortable but signs of movement leaning in Spring's direction.

Most often, I only notice looking back how many small movements have come together to help me find Spring—a moment, a place, or a season in which my larger self has found a chance to emerge. Every poem that follows offers one more example of such moments, a single low-pulsed boom or some small melting toward greening shores. The opening section of poems, *Ice Break,* speaks to the importance of being patient with the long process of melting toward the truth and wholeness we desire.

After the opening section, the collection unfolds into five more. Each explores one aspect of my life that has affected me most deeply:

> *Anima.* According to Jung, the appearance of feminine energy invites the male soul into a greater state of balance (for women, the parallel would be the appearance of *Animus*). The poems in this section reflect my encounters with beauty and love incarnate.

> *Holy Listening.* As a spiritual director, I have experienced the compassion that wells up when we lean into the stories of others with care. A decade of hearing rich stories about life, death, and resurrection has taught me to cherish the unending mysteries of God's love made visible in everyday lives.

> *Yokefellows.* This section pays tribute to the virtues of collaboration and some of the most central partners to my journey. These people have taught me to love people. With them, I continue to learn belonging and humility, mutuality and shared purpose by working shoulder to shoulder toward a common good.

Before God. This section of poems explores prayerfulness as it is practiced intentionally in candled hours of the morning, and also unexpectedly in mystical moments of surprise. These poems remind me to bring my loves to God in whatever state I find them.

Woodland Love. These poems reflect most significantly our family's love for a modest tree farm in Southeast Minnesota that we have been nursing back to health. In that place I hear most clearly and most often a call to intimacy through natural and irrefutable beauty.

As I look back over the ten years in which these poems have been written, what has been melting me closer to the flowing waters of who I am is more gentle and more durable than anything I could have imagined. In love and through loving, I learn to set down my rigid masks and order my life according to a wellspring of compassion and hope. I cannot force or control these loves. Instead, these persistent gifts appear as moments of grace, over and over inviting me to simply see and accept. Sometimes loves show me my belonging in God's light. Sometimes loves show me my shadows. So, I keep writing to linger with them, however those loves stir.

I cannot guarantee that these poems will affect the long change to which readers aspire any more than I can pretend that writing them has made my loves and truth completely steady in me. But I have brought these poems together as one more witness to the possibility that greater authenticity is worth every single scribble.

I do not imagine a world without ice—nor do I want one. I do long for a world melting toward love, a world in which we stand together in the cool waters, living for greener shores and the arrival wild phlox, raspberries, and the brightest greens of budding trees. May *Ice Break* serve as a reminder that Spring is forever arriving, on the warmth of many holy loves.

20 March 2019
First Day of Spring

I
ICE BREAK
melting toward Spring

Ice Break

On the far edge of winter
a frozen lake quakes and groans
as a warm sunrise hints at Spring.

Its slabbed topwater,
fused by arctic nights,
kept silent vigil until now.

Hear the hard water whisper.
Feel its echoed crack,
the rumble of its low-pulsed boom.

Wait in stillness here
until the heart remembers—
any change sounds like this.

The familiar thaws unevenly,
creaking, groaning toward
open waters and greening shores.

Measure Of Words

What is the measure of words we assemble,
setting strands of letters side by side
over an elegantly empty page?

What is the purpose of penning ideas,
adding yet more comment to humanity's
immeasurable mass of text?

Perhaps it's the gift
unwrapped with joy, used a while,
then passed on for others' good.

Perhaps it's the footprint
a life leaves on the world, the faintest hint
that someone tried to pay attention.

Perhaps it's discovery,
not any one single insight,
but staying always close to questions.

Winepress

Each draft is crafted at a wine press,
where bushels of words harvested
from a vineyard ripe with many more
are heaped inside a worn opening,
crowded carefully and pressed together
by a long, slow force of will.
Then, like a trickle of thick crimson,
a paragraph or two seeps through
the narrowest of stained cracks.

Then you wait.

Unseen sugars break down,
fermenting words into something
familiar yet entirely new.
Days become weeks as ideas
vigorously, then gently refine.
Every line began with a yes—
a yes to the harvest,
then to the pressing,
then to the waiting.

In time you will taste the wisdom:
young wines bold and wild,
old wines aged with longsuffering genius.

Moment Of Grace

For a moment I feel alive,
awakened to a mystery
otherwise hidden
by all that is not silence.

For a moment I trust the holy,
breathing warmly, softly,
doubts lifting kindly,
shadows yielding to dawn.

Only a hint of fear remains,
a lingering sense
that this moment will fade,
I will too soon forget.

So I scratch some lines,
a slight remembrance,
calling to my future self from
the beauty of a moment's grace.

True Rising

I have this fear
that when I stop performing
someone will notice
or, worse, not at all.
The script has been simple:
for merits and affection,
achieve, impress, please.
To ease my fear
and face true change
silence must strip me
of masks and images
even I have come to believe.
Do I yet dare
to grieve a lost script,
enter the bareness of hope,
and meet whatever rises
as genuine and worth
becoming?

As A Shadow

As I face the setting Sun,
she casts a long shadow
of the man I want to be.

Brightness makes clear
what does not belong,
reveals clarity and depth.

Sure and ever-faithful,
at times cloud-hidden,
never truly absent.

Little fear of darkness,
sinking calmly into
grace-filled unknowns.

Devoted to dusk
with a heart always
reaching east.

Scripts

What do our souls learn
from stories spoken inwardly
over and over again?

Refrains about being right
and getting our due
make us good at feeling lonely,
nearly as well as lines
about not being enough
and needing to please
teach us to dismiss sheer joy.

So how do we
let go such mischief?
What can we practice
until our hearts warm with virtue?

Perhaps we pray for
freedom from inner untruths,
strength to speak the highest road,
hearts tuned to beauty,
or a long memory
for every instance of grace.

Maybe even turning
toward prayer is the beginning
of a story closer to light
and hope and love.

Wet Wood

A night warms slowly
when winter rains soak
split wood close at hand.
Should you choose not
to search out dry stacks,
fumble along like this:
Begin by pretending
your armload's not that wet.
Double your kindling
and set the logs as always.
Strike your match believing
the small stuff
will dry the rest . . . enough.
Ignore the heavy chimney air
pressing down into the room.
Smoke and sizzle
must mean progress.
More kindling.
More smoke.
Just keep trying
until at last the chill
wears down false logic,
helping you choose the end goal
over convenience,
wisdom set ablaze.

Being Song

Melodies of who I am
are wandering and afraid,
enduring each day
until I come to sleep.

Descants of who I want to be
cause me to rise before dawn,
hoping the night has brought
the strength to change.

When the measures seem
unyielding,
I long for real
harmonies.

Give me a heart
pulsing with beauty
and this holy refrain
—all my being is song.

Maybe This Time
a blessing from Bitrus

Come toward the high altar
to kneel for absolution,
even if you walk distractedly
between pews
over old worn carpet.

Make your way toward
promises of newness and life,
even as yet unaware
a Nigerian clergyman
will lay hands upon your soul.

Let him set a palm gently to each shoulder,
cup them in his warm hands,
not too widely or too high,
but precisely in that place where
bodies join rituals beyond time.

Wait, wait as he, barely moving,
caressing your back,
invites you to absorb a holy calm,
speaking unhurried words
toward healing all anxiety.

Open your heart to the moment,
this sacred opening
to an other-worldly sensation
less like goosebumps than
the skin's strange glow that follows.

Release the words now spoken
—part rubric, part intercession
filled with African love for dear ones—

for they will fade long before your body lets go
the tingling memory of his hands still there.

Welcome new awareness
—this night is unlike all others.
When his last words ring in your ears, *Go and sin no more*,
be ready. For then the whole body's, *Amen*
may mean heartedly, *Maybe this time I can.*

Horizons

As if closing in against a stiff wind,
we fold our whole vision
into the ground beneath our plodding.

Still, something deep refuses
the contortion of high hopes and long views.
A larger self wants to lift up its gaze.

For this we were made—
to plod, to stumble,
and to lift our sights once again.

Embrace any holy glimmer,
for such moments unbend the back,
and clear the scales from our eyes.

Decembers

Time does not depend on our mindfulness.
It impels us without a second's hesitation,
to participate in a single unfolding mystery
through the lens of our one particular life
for as many Decembers as we might see.

II
ANIMA
welcoming the feminine

Anima

Find a humble place
and make your home there.

Can you see the mountains,
the flowers?

Can you hear the waters
flowing?

Prefer not fear and worry
to life and beauty.

Soften, soften.
Let some things fall.

Hold nothing but light.
We are one, you and me.

Writing With Jazz

Confidence rises like a trumpet,
less like reveille than a trellis
on which all else grows.
The trumpet's voice lifts a line
which carries the bright cymbal,
the flittering flute, and the
synthesizer mimicking
violins and organs.

How are we like trumpets,
bravely pressing
breath through cold brass,
our lips and valves
interrupting silence
with some possibility
for others to share?

Like trumpets we are
never really solo.
We rest in others'
willingness to riff
and we ride discoveries
not one of us
could create alone.

Writing With Swing

Joy can be stored
in instruments
and explode into life
when staccato brass
and cymbals steady
burst wide a space
for clarinet and sax
to swing.
Joy beckons
to some seed of itself
in those who hear,
tapping feet
and bobbing heads
giving way
to full-bodied dance.

Awaken

Under the moon's kind quiet
we may not cherish
what stirs us from heavy sleep.

Yet as the sun rises
we yearn for every moment
that opens our hazy eyes.

Welcome, splash of flavor
and dash of surprise.

Welcome, wind in tall grass
and child's pure laugh.

Welcome, oil on canvas
and soul-tuned melodies.

Welcome, hand-written notes
and stories stealing away hurry.

Welcome, new love of old things.

Welcome, numb-piercing sorrow
and brightness that cheers.

Welcome, challenge and possibility
with other sure companions.

Within this new day
and all the moments it brings,

Welcome, welcome,
any fullness of life that wakes us.

Rainbow's Invitation

Across the tarmac
at rain's edge,
a fresh new pallet
gently swells.
The waking sun
grows brighter tones
until even violets shine.
Rainbowed hues
now inspire
every puddle,
every fuselage.
How can we not stop
to drink in this marvel?
How can we not turn
from our travels,
press our hands to the glass,
and gasp in praise?
Calm colors quietly persist,
pooling for a moment
just over there.
See me, they say.
Love.
Remember
as we fade away.

Welcome The Little Children

for Sue

Jesus said,
Welcome the little children,
adding nothing about
age, pigment or language.
So Jesus must have meant those
immune to the drumbeat of time,
those who hold your hand
lest they stray while at wonder,
who squeal with full-bodied joy
at sequins and cardinals,
who get lost in stories,
love naps and snacks,
and who assume friendship
long before introductions.
While they inhabit
the world's hurt like all the rest,
children cannot resist living
by a bigger grace and love.
The kingdom of heaven
belongs to such as these.

She A Tree

Were she to be
only one tree
in the great forest,
she'd first imagine
a walnut.
Tall and worthy,
a hardwood made
for legacy.
Ebony at depth,
reaching out
to nourish the living
all winter.
But soon she'd
remember
her reddened heart,
Spring blossoms,
sweet juice dripping
from songbird beaks
in her branches.
She'd pause and smile,
Wild cherry for me.

Two Wings

for the Missionary Benedictine Sisters
in Daegu, South Korea

Black and white make one
on the wings of magpies
gliding from maple tops to statues
then swiftly down to the grass.
Dissimilar things also comingle
within the monastery nearby—
full habits and tennis shoes,
bright flowers on marbled stone,
square bricks set in the round,
dark stained glass aglow in the sun,
hands calloused in herbal gardens
opening softly in prayer,
sing-song speech becoming one-note chants—
These faithful ones stand
on the sacrifice of their ancestors,
tend the dreams of future generations,
and model a way that awakens
the quiet dignity between all things.
For two wings only fly, says Sister Isaac,
if joined by the love of God.
One wing holds hard truths, sorrow and pain,
the other, virtues soft as hope and trust.
A single wing without the other,
detached from the love of God,
shares no real hope to fly.

Two Waters

for Beth

She says he is a river,
ever flowing downstream,
pressing on to what comes next.

She sees herself
a lake calm and clear,
basking beneath sun and moon.

Both signs of natural order,
though honest ways to live,
carry their own dangers.

His currents may one day slow—
will she still be seen
on the upstream horizon?

Her eye may turn inward—
will she be as much at ease, then,
with what lies within her depths?

To preserve some symbiosis,
the river must learn to yield,
the lake to test its shore's reach.

Trust this comingling,
waters feeding waters,
sharing one common source.

Enough
a dream of mystical union

Alone in darkness
I fail to sleep,
not yet knowing
I long for someone.
Enters my beloved,
lying down beside me,
facing away.
To be near her is enough.

But she stirs and laughs.
When I laugh at her laughing,
she rolls toward me,
my outstretched arm.
I ease my fingers
through the hair behind her ear.
She nestles her soft jaw into my palm.
With regard for nothing more,
we rest in tenderness
until I drift to sleep.
To hold her is enough.

But I wake to making
the love of perfect union
—warm, slow, moving toward
but not beyond
the height of natural oneness.
I see her eyes, dimly,
her perfect chest.
I whisper something about beauty
and wanting this
never to end,
words missing the mark of this

—a rare and wholesome
completion, belonging
found inside another.
Never to be repeated,
never again required,
this night's knowing is enough.

Love Chooses You

after John O'Donohue's Anam Cara

No one controls another's love. We cannot give birth to their affection any more than we can steal it away. Love is ancient and unquestioned oneness over which our striving has no power. So what makes *I love you* slow to pass from ear to heart? Surprise that love has claimed us, doubt the lover has factored in our salty faults, fear of things beyond our schemes, or just underestimating the relentless abiding of true love? When another's fierce tenderness captures you in its gaze, dare to trust the gift of conditionless belonging as surely as you trust the words *I love you* that pulse effortlessly from your heart, across your lips, and toward the object of your own deepest longing and highest loyalty, the love exceeding your every purpose and delight.

III
HOLY LISTENING
leaning into stories

Holy Listening

Life's noise sometimes
buries the voice of love,
leaving the more timid
slow to speak of God.
But when you offer
kind stillness,
the meek can brave
clumsy words,
awkward pauses,
images still unclear.
Listen heartfully
near this tomb,
for the stone
      is rolling away.

Being Heard

Though we toss words
in hopes that intention
lands well for listeners,
we never know for sure
until someone leans in,
asks a real question
or recounts something
we said that she
refused to forget.
In the heat of true
understanding,
words rekindle their magic
and our passion to speak
catches fire.

Being Seen

When a woman
wears polka dots,
people presume
she is happy.
When she wears black,
they often ask
if it's for show.
A nobler story lives
beyond mere clothing,
one of complex beauty
beneath her skin.
She wants eyes opened
to her life of fierce
integrity.
Then, feeling truly seen,
her fears loosen
and she becomes
courage adorned.

Dear Listener

by Zoe Rahberg (age 14) with Samuel Rahberg

Some things make me want to push back.

> If you tell me I want to,
> I don't.
> If you tell me I shouldn't,
> I might.
> If you tell me I can't,
> just watch me.

Some things draw me in.

> If you tell me you're with me,
> that helps.

> If you tell me you believe in me,
> I feel encouraged.

> And when I ask you to sit and listen,
> don't try to fix things for me . . .
> Just sit
> and listen.

Some things require a redo.

> Don't tell me how I feel.
> Don't judge my right and wrong.
> And when you find yourself saying,
> If I were you . . .
> please try again.

Dear friend,
just listen.

Not Alone

We may presume to know
what preachers mean by Gospel,
assenting to notions of Jesus,
grace and elegant words
sung, recited and prayed

While we trudge on lonely paths
through clouds of doubt and shame,
through inner fogs of fear and pain
so thick they conceal our bondage,
so thick we lose our way.

Until we witness grace first-hand:
a man glimpsing his true self,
a woman starting to wear red again,
a saddened soul stirring toward joy;
the meek finally feeling heard.

Then comes true light into the world.
Then breaks into the heart's real knowing
what has been declared time and again,
what this God intends by Incarnation—
We are not alone. We are not alone.

A Healing Sadness

for the Vaudt family

When sickness enters the body,
instinct summons every cell,
channels a person's whole strength
toward well-being restored.

So, too, the nature of sadness,
a soul's deliberate slowing,
an attentive solitude
impossible to ignore.

Though weak and wearied,
trust healing will come,
in its own time,
and has already begun.

And when it seems too much,
when you can do no more than lie still
with closed eyes and shallow breath,
let it be enough, then, to wait.

Drawn from Rainer Maria Rilke's eighth letter in *Letters to a Young Poet*. (Merchant Books, 2012).

Damp Inside

What becomes of dark stories
first absorbed apart
from one's own choosing,
then harbored in memory unawares?
Unlike roaring waves crashing,
these tales seep in unnoticed.

They pool until they spill,
reaching long fingers under walls,
touching the bottoms of upright beams.
They creep up the grain,
dampen wood's strength
and hide there,
soaking walls inside-out,
making mold and odor
grow together contently.

When found at last
behind stain or smell,
throw open the window,
even if you still yield
to the damage that remains.

Light, light
is the deeper cure.
Tear off the walls,
expose the frame.
Shine, shine
upon the source
that it may be seen and ceased.
Let sun and breeze disinfect
while you rebuild
what should not be rotted.

There now, begin again.

The Trickster

What mischief rises in the night
when everyone else is sleeping?
The house quiet, neighbors locked in,
the city's hum set to dim.

An unwelcome guest begins to stir,
tossing the mind, turning the body.
Too hot?, *Too cold?*, it whispers and grins,
Something forgotten? or *Too much said?*

This trickster robs sleep
with hints and half-truths,
content to amuse itself
in spaces emptied of day.

Press it away or chase its lures
and fall further yet from sleep.
Or, let it come and wander away
like smoke into darkness
      over a wick burned out.

103 Korean Martyrs

Hard stories make strong children
where mountains still whisper
in the Land of the Morning Calm.

Remember those who sought
and found a way of joy
surpassing the fear of death.

Thousands were crushed
when fierce bonds of love
threatened the social order.

Inscribe on your hearts
these ancestors' names
because they held firm.

Learn their courage to brave mountains,
to etch crosses into kimchi jars,
to keep daring for love.

During the nineteenth century the Christian church in Korea endured four major persecutions as thousands died for their faith. 103 of these faithful women and men were canonized by John Paul II in 1984. The vitality of today's Korean church is inextricably linked to their faithful witness.

Seoul Vespers

When pilgrims hear only music
in language that means something
to those who live here,
there is no choice but to feel
the way into prayer.
One can watch for the right time
to rise, to bow, to sit.
One can listen for the lilt
of psalms, hymns and readings.
One might even glean a
Christo, *Maria* or *Amen*,
as clear young voices
chant in single tones.
Like the winged choir perched
on Asian pines nearby,
pilgrim hearts draw in close,
moved beyond listening,
unable to resist the song.

¡Más Mezcla!

for Habitat Paraguay

¡Más mezcla!,
the masons cry
and we mix sand,
soil and cement.
Water dipped from drums
pail by pail.

So many bricks.
So much mortar.
Pail by pail
we dry up
a family's
only drinking,
only washing.

Toma la agua,
the mother says,
risking all
to set a new
foundation
   —for my childrens.

Tonight she will
go to the stream,
pail by pail,
starting again
toward survival.

Tomorrow,
¡Más mezcla!,
and we will again
risk with her
to build her
children a home.

Carmen was the name of the mother
for whom volunteers from Thrivent
Builds and Habitat for Humanity were
working in a rural village of Paraguay,
well outside the capital city of
Asunción. *Mezcla* is Spanish for the *mix*
used as mortar; *Toma the aqua* means
Take the water.

Here In Wales

Skies weep until light
widens across the land.
Hills stand still
like the stones
nestled within them,
erected upon them.
Sheep graze faithfully,
cattle climb bravely,
castles and abbeys
rise and crumble
while poets and peasants
preach stories without end.
All things speak Christ.
All things express
one eternal Word.
And speak they must,
for in this place,
all things reveal its soul.

Learning Lectio
From An Old Welsh Cow

Slow and steady
tear the grass
grind, grind
iron jaws
keep chewing
drop down
pulling, pulling
raise head
chewing, looking
pause
watch
chewing, chewing
swat tail
pulling, pulling
tongue out
snort, snort
chewing, chewing
stand still,
lift tail
lose patty
chewing, chewing
pulling, pulling
all day long

Living Stones

Some people like to move the earth, level the ground, and build a politely square box to serve as home or church. The Welsh teach another way, wrapping buildings around trees and over contours that long endure. Mortar crumbles, wood rots, paint surely peels. The land models a conversion and stability far more dependable than mortal schemes. Cathedrals live as long as humans exert their will over them, driving away rain and vandals. And when there are too few Pounds Sterling, Euros, or Dollars? One hundred years will bring a sanctuary to its knees. Two hundred will bury it. And yet the hills will thrive as they rise up beneath the walls, giving creatures like us a real place to stand . . . at least for a time. For, one day, we too will return to dust and become bits for stone. Then, some pilgrim will pick us up, speak of Christ, and carry us along a new way.

IV
YOKEFELLOWS
learning mutuality

Yokefellows

Philippians 4:3

A yoke lets the full burden
be shared for just a while.
Remember this when the task
proves too much to go alone.

The yoke itself,
worn smooth by practice,
holds the memory
of every load set in motion.

So, too, all yokefellows
who learn to share the load,
lean against the impossible,
feeling it give way.

Call Me By Name

for Carol

Call me by name,
not by some title
to flatter me
or get me to do
whatever it is you want.
I have heard
a lifetime of sounds,
learning to cherish
one voice above all,
a voice that comes in whispers,
a voice that comes in storm.
I listen for the one
who has always led me,
calling me by name.

Breadth Of Heaven

for Uncle Paul

Some men inspire us,
not by ordinary valor or charm,
but by unpolished authenticity.

Absent are the trappings
of inflated personas
and the predictability of etiquette.

These men laugh deeply, live loudly,
not to meet anyone's expectations
but to live with pure primal force.

For us to avert our eyes from them
is merely to deny our own
shadows politely tucked away.

Like Psalmists and jesters of old,
these men dare to do otherwise,
belting their curses and praises out loud.

They live through their choices,
bearing repeated witness
to the profusion of God's grace.

Give thanks for men like these
who show the breadth of heaven.

Uncle Paul liked to say about his brother, my father, *Dave can show you how to get to heaven; I can show you the rest!*

The Smell Of Poverty

When we all said yes
the task seemed simple.
Complexities only grew
after parking downtown
and searching out one room
among a high rise of the same,
each hiding a story of its own.

As 907 opened the reek
of rotten meals and sordid clothes
rolled out in waves.
Garbage lay where it fell.
Worn furniture crammed in,
a dresser, an end table,
a chair used for a bed.

He knelt there,
disheveled as his surroundings,
shuffling small things,
looking up to say quietly
he was surprised we actually came.
Our eagerness muted
by depression's stench.

We had forty minutes
to gather his belongings,
get them to public storage.
When we fumbled, he assured us
he needed very little,
not even a change of clothes,
and yes, he would be alright
after his midnight eviction.

We set about the task,
with all our ranks and privileges,

each one knowing
that for all our power
we were not as strong
as the smell of poverty
and the ache of human need.

Straight Talk

When two people are hidden
from each other
by the debris
of unspoken opinions,
stories and expectations,
they might prefer
to leave things be,
silent and alone,
settled in a narrowed view.
Except the other side
cannot really be denied.
Ignore it, stew about it,
or risk the conversation.
Only risk holds possibility.
Call out to the unknown,
speak your truth,
listen and remove
one obstacle at a time.
Whatever the cost,
talk your way home
to a truly common good.

True Partners

Sit down with a true partner,
meet vulnerability with openness,
ambiguity with patience,
conflict with underlying love.

Stand up with a true partner,
speak convictions out loud
with passion and purpose
sharing one voice.

Walk with a true partner,
finding your pace
with eyes on one horizon
step after step.

Embody together
intimacy, courage,
and trust.

Work Of Belonging

The impulse for work
dwells in a primal place
near the human instincts
for warmth and food.

So labor serves
our common needs
for survival,
for belonging.

Along our way
we encounter
people and yearnings
wanting to be seen.

We bond with them
when we choose
to notice and engage,
lending them our lives.

We find together
that every simple
act participates
in making our world.

The best work, then,
helps us discover
we are warmed in this doing
and hungry for even more.

Roofing Together

The online world makes us
hungry for sore hands, sweat,
and the taste of progress

The kind of work easier
to begin than finish,
the stuff of proud stories.

But can we still labor,
muscles atrophied
by keyboards and screens?

Let us come with ladders
and shingles and climb,
climb to the challenge.

Breathe deep
and rekindle the body's
appetite for hard use.

Here we shoulder together
the task not one of us
could accomplish alone.

Stoking The Fire
for Victor

To stoke a fire is the
most ancient petition
made for those who do not stir.

The call to prayer begins
with a chill, an invitation
soon irresistible.

You rise alone,
slipping from slumber
toward the hearth's fading warmth.

There, peering into red-orange coals,
you meet the hope of the whole home
for something more.

Take one or two tokens
of the family's anticipation,
dry oak cut, split, and stacked.

Kneel as mothers and watchmen
from every age, opening the stove
and making your simple offering.

No one will see to thank you
but the shadows and the sounds
who likewise go unnoticed.

Stay now at the warming fire,
or yield this vigil to the night,
and rejoin your sleeping loves.

Dreamers And Parents
for Levi Oluafemi

We give birth to dreams and children,
mysteries passing through us,
carrying forward our best, bright sparks.

We lose sleep for them,
our first thoughts upon waking
and our prayers into the night.

We feed them with abandon
not simply to quiet their cries,
but to nourish hopes that they might grow.

All the while the world turns on,
full of dreamers and parents
living with hearts wide open.

With One Voice

Some days the monastic choir voice cracks,
like when Sister Pat intones the hymn off-key,
sending both sides straining for pitch
and wandering up and down the scale.

Or when spoken psalms stutter,
with fewer Sisters ready to pray,
some still shuffling in,
others falling asleep.

We the guests now need to choose—
to become bothered, to strive for harmony,
to let go our expectations,
to grieve signs of diminishment.

Or we can choose to be present
while faithful women catch their breath,
lending our voices to lift petitions
they have carried for the world

Three times a day, for seventy years.
We may not be here at Vigils,
they may not be here tomorrow,
but for now, let us pray.

Feet First

Those who wade swift waters
know the thunderous roar of currents
pressing so hard against balance
that blue waters break white.

Those brave souls practice setting
one foot carefully after the next,
working down through loose stones
toward something more solid.

When the current takes them
—and it sometimes will—
they turn feet first
in order to survive.

They do not flail madly
or swim against the river's strength.
They yield and focus until
the river lets them go.

V
BEFORE GOD
practicing prayerfulness

Before God

after an Orthodox anthology, The Art of Prayer

Thoughts jostle one another
  like swarming gnats,
emotions make them swell.

I long for an inner
  turning toward God,
a secret dwelling,
    constant aliveness.

I want to root my life
  in a sense of God
that directs all things.

I imagine myself
  plunged deep in love,
truly free and collected.

Such a turn calls for
  something beyond my power,
so I ask, Lord Christ,
  for your presence.

As I await your Spirit
  and the next warm call
to serve, to love

Help me stand
  with mind in heart
before God.

Ceaseless Prayer

What is the point of discipleship
if not to live truthfully
in the Divine Presence?

To saturate ourselves
with Scripture that we
might dwell in the Word

That centeredness might
well up as sacred stories
claim our hearts and minds

That fullness of soul
might spill over into
faith and hope and love

So the way of prayer
might not be confined
to candled moments at dawn.

Dear God

I am coming to see
that those I serve
are not my own but
infinitely complex
persons being drawn
into mystery.
I am like them,
yet singular,
connected,
but still not fused.
In you I belong
completely,
not grasping
but abiding
in that place where
desires are born,
passions are forged.
Let me not lose
sight of these things,
for in my being
and my doing
I sometimes forget
first and always
we are entirely thine.

Sit With Me

for Nathanael

This is the morning
I am ready
to quiet old worries,
offer them up.
Tired of trying
new schemes,
I purpose one more—
I'll pray through weakness.

Before I can begin,
a child comes,
Daddy, Daddy,
can I sit with you?
He climbs to my lap
and reads to himself
of sea creatures,
ones with weird eyeballs.
He sniffles and
wiggles and warms me.

God's swift reply—
Be not alone.

Inkling

Desiring God seems simple enough,
but today I can't quite
glimpse the divine.

I envy Oliver's white fire,
Hopkins' holy grandeur,
Whyte's center of longing.

But when the wise in spirit say
the ordinary itself is enough,
I feel the imposter.

Too hard at the grind,
too long at the rush,
I am left numb to the Presence.

When the sun rises on a new day,
I pray, Quiet God,
give me an inkling.

Next Thing

When I am here,
it is there.
When I am now,
it is then.
The next bite,
a perfect morsel.
The next project,
a worthy difference.
The next friend,
a better companion.
Next, next, meaning
this, this is never
quite enough.
Maker of moments,
ease my drivenness.
Teach me how
to love this
here and now.

Lukewarm
Revelation 3:15-22

Neither too hot nor too cold
is the greater danger
to common life.
Hot heads fuel fear,
cold hearts corrupt harmonies,
yet nothing rots covenants
like lukewarm indifference.

Behold, the Holy One calls,
I stand at the door and knock.

We may not have
the fire to drive him away
nor the ice to refuse him,
but let us not be caught
humming to ourselves,
pretending he's not there.

Set down tepid ways,
put a hand to the latch.

Farmers Sing

They sing their *Amens*
in full harmony,
sounding their trust that again
there will be enough for winter.

Hymnals fall open to familiar pages,
worn thin by thick, calloused hands,
the same ones that built this chapel
and still tinker with the boiler.

With homesteaders gone,
great-grandchildren leaving,
the air is tired as dusk.
And yet they sing, faithful as a field
bearing season after season.

Signs Of Hope

upon the baptism of Noah Adedeji

Time turns on holy moments,
moments like these.
Swaddled ones, simple fonts,
young and old stretching to see
water cascading,
tender anointing.

We all want grace,
some vision to redeem
what we could not,
some stalwart promise
of God claiming,
Christ dwelling.

God Made Known
for Chance | John 1:18

The real danger in growing up
is forgetting how to wonder.
You were born knowing to play,
explore, and follow curiosity
toward mysteries.
When you grow older,
and duty starts to outweigh joy,
remember this—
the only Son,
close to the Father's heart,
cannot resist seeking you,
making God known to you
and this whole marvelous world.

Grace Upon Grace
for Gabriel | John 1:16

When the world tells you
who you are and what you have
is not quite enough

That you should be taller,
your car should be faster,
your wealth always more

When the world tells you
to fight and cling and protect
whatever small portion is yours

Remember this—
God is wildly generous,
lavishing love on you.

This grace beyond abundance
holds all you really need—
unfailing, unending love.

Seeing God
Matthew 5:8

pure hearts
see God

seems old,
distant truth
    thankfully

for if my depths
were simple,
    free

love might
busy me
    with silence

or
    consume me

Death Before Our Eyes

Christian journey soon be over . . .

Freedom glimmers
at seeing an end, not to moments,
but to the journey itself.

Striving will cease.
All building, resolving
will come to an end.

Somehow, awakened to death,
we can live more deeply
into the truth that sets free.

For the end is not about fear
but the urgent invitation
to live this day to the full.

VI
WOODLAND LOVE
engaging nature's beauty

Woodland Love

There is a beauty to these woods
that surpasses even the twilight
sound of the Great Horned Owl
or the crescent moon spilling stars
onto cedar tops and pines.

These woods grow inside me
with the long call of possibility.
Nature remains unhurried
as water and wind form the habits
of countless species, and me.

Even as I stand able to dream
within the forest's seasons;
my own life will measure
only a few dense rings hidden
deep inside mighty oaks.

However long my days,
I cannot forget these woods.
Near or far they enliven
my wondering and hoping
and choosing.

First Snow

Snow falls on the woods
while children lie on their backs
and gentleness kisses the earth.

Soon will come
stomping, rolling, tossing,
—but not quite yet.

This is the
moment for marvel,
a tithe of winter's first fruits.

Before mittens
grow heavy and toes
start to numb

Souls must swell to wonder
at God repainting the world
one flake at a time.

Night Chorus

Some nights the mind can't tell
waking thoughts from chorus frogs.
While all is dull
but the hearth's crackle,
a stirring chorus begins.
One frog wakens others
in undulating rhythms,
tapering off after a time.
Gently one trills
and waits, waits
until the chorus swells again.
What causes the mind to rise?
Frog song piercing the silence
or thoughts swelling in chorus,
the ribbets of one's own
wonderings?
In the deep dark of night,
such are the curiosities
that bother a mind
just trying to sleep.

Skunk Hollow Sunrise

Darkness fades now, awakening
long wrinkled faces of oaks
stretching up from the coulee.
Can you find calm enough
to let their leaves settle
and the squirrel rustle,
while the grass sways
and the field mouse wanders
up onto your boot?
Can you wait without flinching,
so you can make out
the goose, the cardinal,
and the tap-tapping nut hatch?
Listen through the steady white noise
until you hear handfuls of stream
pressing over certain smooth stones.
Only then, tuned to subtlety
and the sun's glow crawling
down the woodlands,
will the twig-snap
and the low, uneven thud
of heavy footsteps
show you the wild doe.

Wait, Be Still

Have you ever waited so long
that gray squirrels come close
and with blackened paws
show you how they shuck
walnuts with their teeth?

Have you been so still
that red squirrels perch
on the log beside you,
peeling scales from pinecones
—bottom to top—
until only a stem remains?

It makes me wonder
what wisdom might appear
if we could simply wait
and be still.

Just Breathe

eyes fix
ears snap
just as
lungs pull down
air tight
heart slams
stiff still

just breathe

let go
gently
smoothly

through
trembling
draw in

open
easy
loosen

focus
calm

breathe

Taking The Shot
for Denny

The most seasoned hunter
settles in early,
   ready to wait hours upon hours,
       moon after moon,
for something to slip
   quietly into view.

When at last it comes,
   stiffly and slowly,
he draws the full weight of the bow
   across his back,
holds aim on a small patch of soft hide.

Before growing unsteady,
   he must weigh
       life and death.

Years in the open air
   at once cold, wet, and satisfied,
have honed his courage to choose:
   Let fly today, or
       wait again tomorrow.

These are moments to live for,
   some carefully scouted,
most whispered calls
       to adventure.

The prayerful listen and watch
       and feel each day
for stirrings of God—
   eternities marked by seconds—
       and the heart says, *Yes*.

The Hunt

I do not love
the kill and carcass.
I love climbing a bluff
before sunrise and waiting
for mourning doves
to root beneath dry leaves,
pileated woodpeckers
to drum upright logs,
cool breeze
to carry away flies,
red fox
to trot by within reach,
and then
the doe.
An arrow,
a long silence,
waiting for what I love more—
prayers of thanks
to rise through woods,
loved ones
to work with me,
to dance with me,
to share a meal with story.

The Long Wind
after John Muir's A Wind-Storm in the Forest

A soft breeze slips by unnoticed
until a leaf dances across grass
or white pine limbs sway.

A hard gust demands respect
until we bow into it
or get pressed away.

Although they seem fleeting,
the breeze, the gust,
local spirits swirling nearby

These are long winds,
rising up before time,
lifting oceans over deserts
over woods.

Noble Oaks

A royal family of ancient trees
    holds court late one autumn.

Velvet browns, old yellows,
    and the green of sages
    gather around a long
    line of reds deep as merlot.

Lesser groves
    surround them,
    all bright colors spent.

These nobles stand
    at sky's rim,
    waiting to bow down.

When The Oaks Fall

Old trees crown the forest
over a dense swarm
of newcomers.
Something dark-scaled,
feigning black cherry,
already crowds
the lower limbs of giants.
Do not stand by idly,
or, when someday fall
the towering few,
we will all, like logs
left to decay, look up
to see buckthorn
inherit the crown.

Trees Planted By Streams
Psalm 1

A tree planted by cool waters
sinks its roots deep into moist soil,
drawing life from the stream
while holding firm the banks.

It is called to gaze upon
the flowing mystery
arriving from somewhere unseen,
leading to somewhere unknown.

This tree is called to press down
toward hidden stability,
growing stronger
by one ring each year.

There will be calm days
void of any breeze,
others with soft, stirring winds,
surely some with gale force.

As long as this tree lives,
whatever any season brings,
its work remains the same:
grow deep and wide

Reach upward, make leaves
—even knowing they will fall—
keep gazing upon the stream
that carries you into mystery.

Legacy

Memorials and headstones
are too obvious.
Give me something simple,
like a path gently worn
through bluffland woods.

Let those who follow walk
beneath tall cedars,
where sounds and textures
so enchant them
that the way itself
goes unnoticed.

When they find friendship
with that holy place,
let them remember
the one who lived,
who dreamed, who made
this path, step by step.
Let them set their minds
to long kinship
and keeping the way
for those yet to come.

And if none follow,
I will still rest in peace
knowing this path will return
to the same lush wild
through which I walked
and found
beauty surpassing
the finest etched granite.

ABOUT THE AUTHOR

Samuel Rahberg is a husband and a father of two who has been working with poetry for over ten years. He is author of *Enduring Ministry: Toward a Lifetime of Christian Leadership* (Liturgical Press, 2017) and *The Gospels in Poem and Image* (with Natalie Rahberg, Aetos Publications).

Samuel serves as a spiritual director in Saint Paul and as Director of the Benedictine Center of St. Paul's Monastery. He holds a Master of Arts in Theology from Saint John's School of Theology and Seminary (Collegeville, MN).

For the joy of encountering God in nature, Samuel and his family own and manage a woodland retreat in Southeast Minnesota.

info@samuelrahberg.com

www.samuelrahberg.com

www.facebook.com/samuelrahberg

www.ingramcontent.com/pod-product-compliance
Lightning Source LLC
Chambersburg PA
CBHW071149090426
42736CB00012B/2288